Copyright © 2017 by Lenn Vincent GmbH.

All rights reserved. This book or any portion thereof may not be reproduced or used in any manner whatsoever without the express written permission of the publisher except for the use of brief quotations in a book review.

First Printing, 2017

ISBN 978-3-9524827-9-7

www.leosnowpard.com

Leo Snowpard
AND HIS FIRST DONATION

Author
MELANIE ROEMER

Illustrations by
JUN-PIERRE SHIOZAWA

Leo and his family want to go to the lake together today. But unfortunately it is raining heavily this Sunday afternoon.

Together, they think about what they can do. Leo's daddy has an idea. "What do you think about transforming our living room into an atelier and paint beautiful pictures." Leo's dad is not just a great entrepreneur, he is also a great artist.

Leo thought briefly. Perhaps he is also such a super artist like his dad. "Oh yes. Maybe my pictures look as beautiful as yours?" Leo's dad smiles and is proud that Leo likes his pictures.

Together, they begin to transform the living room into an atelier. Leo and his mom cover everything that should not get dirty. Leo's dad and Lilly bring brushes, water and everything you need to paint. They even have painting aprons for everyone. Together they paint the whole afternoon until the evening.

"Oh, it's late. Let's clean up and have dinner," says Leo's dad. Together, they clear everything up and put the pictures in the living room.

"Leo, you really painted a very nice picture." Leo's mom praises. Leo is very proud and finds his colorful picture very beautiful.

The next morning, Mrs. Smith, Leo's class teacher, comes to the class with a new boy. "Children, here is Jacob, your new classmate. Jacob, we are glad to have you with us. Why don't you sit down on the free seat up there?" Jacob smiles shyly and sits down at the free place right next to Leo and Maya.
"Hello Jacob, I'm Leo." "And I'm Maya." Leo and Maya greet him.
"Hello," says Jacob shyly.

"Are you new here in the city?" Leo is interested to find out. Jacob is sad. "No. Our house burnt down and we had to move. My favorite bear Bruno and all my toys were also burnt. Now we have no money to buy a new teddy. I miss Bruno so much."

After school, Lilly picks up Leo and they go straight home. Leo thinks about Jacob all the time and how he has lost his favorite teddy bear.

At home, the whole family is already waiting. Leo Snowpard's aunt Tanja is visiting. Aunt Tanja is very interested in Leo's art. "Wow Leo, did you paint this picture? That looks great!" Leo is quite proud and nods. "Say Leo, what do you think about me giving you money for your money box and I can have this great picture?" Leo likes this suggestion.

Leo thinks about Jacob again. "You know Auntie, in my class there is a new boy, Jacob. His house burned down. His whole toys are burned."

"Oh, that's bad." Aunt Tanja says.

Leo continues, "And now his parents have no money to buy anything."
Leo has an idea. "How about I paint several art pictures and sell them? I could use the money to buy Jacob a new Bruno?" Aunt Tanja shines. "That means you want to donate the money that you earn with your artwork to Jacob. That's a great idea, Leo." Aunt Tanja praises Leo. "How about you come to me on Wednesday afternoon. All my girlfriends visit me. If you like, you can show your artwork to them. Maybe one of them will buy a picture."
"That would be great!" says Leo.

Leo paints the next days diligently. Leo enjoys designing new artwork and trying out different colors. Leo's dad looks at the finished pictures. "Well done, Leo, this looks great! Especially this colorful picture, I like it a lot. I would like to keep this one." Leo's dad admires the artwork of Leo Snowpard. "You cannot have this, dad. I need this for the donation for Jacob." In the meantime, Leo has already got a money box from Lilly. So there is no confusion, he wrote "Donation for Jacob" on the outside of the box.

It is Wednesday and Leo goes to Aunt Tanja with all his new artwork. He arrives early to be able to nicely set up his artworks. Then Aunt Tanja's girlfriends arrive. Leo is very shy at the beginning and whispers only "Hello." Suddenly a friend, Rihanna Rhino starts to marvel. "Tanja Snowpard, where did you get this beautiful artwork?"
"They are from my nephew Leo Snowpard. Do you like them?"
"Yes, they are beautiful and so colorful."

Suddenly it spurts out of Leo. "You can buy my artworks. I am collecting money for my friend Jacob. His house burned down and I'd like to buy him a new teddy bear."

And so the girlfriends buy the artwork one after another. Leo is very proud. He sold all of his artwork. When the girlfriends went home, Leo and Aunt Tanja count the money from his donation box. "Yay, Aunt Tanja. I have twelve dollars in my donation box. Is that a lot of money? Do I have enough to buy a Bruno?"

"Yes Leo, that should be enough money."

On the weekend, Jacob is invited to play with Leo. They play together all morning. They get hungry and go to the kitchen. Lilly calls the two of them. "Leo, did you already tell Jacob about your donation box?" Leo shines, he takes Jacob by the hand and runs with him to his room.

Leo excitingly explains to Jacob. "Jacob, I painted artwork and sold them. I collected the money for you in a donation box. With this money I want to buy you a Bruno." "What?" Jacob can hardly believe it.

"Now Lilly and I would like to go with you to a stuffed animal shop and buy one." Jacob is quite shy, but Leo realizes he is happy. Lilly jumps up. "Well, you two, ready to go?" "Yes, for sure." Leo is glad and pulls up Jacob. And they are already on their way to the stuffed animal shop.

Having arrived at the shop, Jacob goes straight to a teddy bear. Leo runs after him. "Would you like this one, Jacob?" "Oh, that would be great. He looks exactly like Bruno," says Jacob. "Then we'll buy him," says Leo.

When they leave the shop, Jacob embraces Leo and thanks him. "Leo, why did you save money for me? You did not have to." Leo smiles and answers, "You were so sad because all your toys and Bruno were burned. I wanted to help you."
Jacob is pleased. And Leo is glad that he could give something to his friend that made him happy. It's fun to do something for others. The two have the idea to work on another donation project together. What it will be? Who knows!

www.ingramcontent.com/pod-product-compliance
Lightning Source LLC
Chambersburg PA
CBHW040034050426
42453CB00003B/112